MW01074854

DWELL
IN THE *Psalms*

FINDING OUR HOME IN GOD'S WORD

A Soul Inspired Bible Study

Dwell in the Psalms—Finding Our Home in God's Word

A Soul Inspired Bible Study Booklet

ISBN: 978-1723823725
Published by: Kindle Direct Publishing

Devotions written by: Mitzi Neely
Illustrations "jlk": Copyright © 2017 Jana Kennedy-Spicer

Cover Design by: Jana Kennedy-Spicer
Interior Design by: Jana Kennedy-Spicer

CONTENTS

dwell / -verb

1. To live or stay as a permanent resident

2. To live or continue in a given condition

3. To linger over or ponder in thought, speech or writing

INTRODUCTION

Let me ask you...

Have you ever been blindsided and hurt by someone?

Have your circumstances ever caused you to loose your joy?

Have you ever felt overwhelmed by a busy life?

Have you ever been disappointed by unanswered prayers?

Umm.. *yes, yes, yes and oh, yes.*

I'm sure we could have answered "yes" to any of these questions at some point or another, for me, it was once all in the same week! - during a particularly busy and stress-filled time amidst a work project which was not at all staying on schedule. It seemed what ever result, assistance or direction for which we prayed, we actually experienced the exact opposite. The joy and excitement which had propelled me into the project had long since faded. Busy and overwhelmed was an understatement as the to-do list grew exponentially each and every day. The results were not as expected and people were disappointed, and that disappointment was heaped on me.

It caused me to once again stop and ask myself why I was doing what I was doing. On the surface that may seem like a good question to dive into, but from my particular perspective, it was more of a challenge to God about why things were turning out so badly if I was going where he said to go and doing what he said to do.

Little did I know just how big that little "if" was. Because God responded with *"are you?"*.

Well what does that mean God? *"Are you 'going where I said to go' and 'doing what I said to do'?"*

This heart-check caused me to pause and reevaluate.

In Luke we learn of two sisters, Mary and Martha.
"Now as they went on their way, Jesus entered a village . And a woman named Martha welcomed him into her house. And she had a sister called Mary, who sat at the Lord's feet and listened to his teaching. But Martha was distracted with much serving. And she went up to him and said, "Lord, do you not care that my sister has left me to serve alone? Tell her then to help me." But the Lord answered her, "Martha, Martha, you are anxious and troubled about many things, but one thing is necessary. Mary has chosen the good portion, which will not be taken away from her." Luke 10:38-42

You may already be familiar with Martha and her sister Mary. If you're like me, you may also be very well acquainted with your inner Martha. For Martha, it wasn't that her serving was bad, but rather that she was more focused on her serving than her guest, Jesus. Who, by the way, had just walked right into the middle of her living room and sat down to spend time with her.

And so was I. .. *more focused on my serving than on Jesus.* In fact I had not sat down and spent any quality time with him in quite awhile... because I was too busy. And too distracted. And too independent.

Have you ever been there? Are you there right now?

If so, then I am so happy you have picked up *"Dwell in the Psalms— Finding Our Home in God's Word"*. This is not another study about our beloved Martha and Mary, but rather a word of encouragement to accept God's invitation to spend time with Him and how doing so can change your life.

My sweet friend, Mitzi Neely from Peacefully Imperfect has joined us to talk candidly about several times in her own life when pausing to spend time with God made a dramatic impact on her personally, professionally, and visibly to those around her.

- *How God Sustains Through Our Circumstances*
- *How to Dwell in Peace When You've Been Sucker-Punched*
- *Dwelling in the Presence of God When You Have a Busy Life*
- *How to Dwell in the Spirit When Disappointment Strikes*

Our prayer is that this devotional book and journal will greatly encourage you in your everyday life as you walk with God.

Before you begin, stop, pause and take time to sit with God. Ask him to speak directly to your heart, making His scriptures personal and pouring the message he has just for you, all over your life.

Blessings Soul Friends, and Let Your Souls be Inspired.

We CAN BE
TIRED, WEARY &
EMOTIONALLY DISTRAUGHT
BUT AFTER
spending time
ALONE WITH
God
WE
FIND THAT
HE injects
OUR BODIES
WITH ENERGY, POWER
& STRENGTH.

CHARLES STANLEY

SCRIPTURE READING LIST

1. Psalm 4:8
2. Psalm 5:4
3. Psalm 15:1
4. Psalm 23:6
5. Psalm 24:1
6. Psalm 25:13
7. Psalm 26:8
8. Psalm 27:4
9. Psalm 37:27
10. Psalm 37:29
11. Psalm 37:3
12. Psalm 39:12
13. Psalm 43:3
14. Psalm 61:4
15. Psalm 65:4
16. Psalm 68:6

17. Psalm 69:35-36
18. Psalm 84:10
19. Psalm 84:4
20. Psalm 85:9
21. Psalm 87:2
22. Psalm 91:1
23. Psalm 98:7
24. Psalm 101:6
25. Psalm 101:7
26. Psalm 107:35-37
27. Psalm 125:1
28. Psalm 132:14
29. Psalm 133:1
30. Psalm 139:9-10
31. Psalm 140:13

How to Use this Study

In this study booklet, you will find four weekly study sections which include:

- Memory Verse & Scripture Reading List
- Devotional + Study Questions
- 3 Scripture Study Pages
- Prayer Journal Page
- Scripture Art Coloring Page

On each of the Scripture Study Pages there are 5 sections to help you dive deeper into God's Word. Select a scripture from the Reading List and complete each section as follows...

READ : Read the scripture. Read it in context including the scriptures before and after, maybe even the whole chapter. Look it up in multiple translations. Then, write out the scripture in your own words, personalizing it specific to you and your current situation.

REFLECT : Use your Bible study sources (commentaries, dictionaries, etc or BibleHub.com) to learn more about the scripture. Make notations about what stood out to you.

RELATE : How does this scripture relate to you personally or your life situation? What does God want you to know from this scripture? How does it speak God's reassurances to you? Make all of these notations in this section.

REMEMBER : What is the one or main thing about the scripture which you want to remember?

PRAY : Conclude your study time by writing a prayer to God. Maybe incorporate portions of the scripture. Praise God and thank Him for the blessings in your life.

Dwell in the Psalms

If you're like me, you may need more writing room, so keep some blank paper handy. Use the blank pages included to study additional scriptures.

My prayer is that this booklet and these devotions will enhance your time spent dwelling with God in His Word.

On the Prayer Journal pages, select one or two of the scriptures from each session to personalize and pray back to God.

Also you'll find lots of space to journal and let your soul be inspired.

FOR BIBLE JOURNALERS

On the back pages of this booklet, you'll find several items which you can color, clip and use in your Bible Art Journaling. There are also scripture coloring pages included throughout.

Prayer Journal

WHAT INSPIRED YOUR SOUL THIS WEEK?

I LOVE YOUR *sanctuary* LORD THE PLACE WHERE *Your* GLORIOUS PRESENCE *dwells.*

PSALM 26:8 NLT

WEEK ONE
Scripture Reading

1 PSALM 4:8

2 PSALM 5:4

3 PSALM 15:1

4 PSALM 23:6

5 PSALM 24:1

6 PSALM 25:13

7 PSALM 26:8

How God Sustains
THROUGH OUR CIRCUMSTANCES

"Send me your light and your faithful care, let them lead me; let them bring me to your holy mountain, to the place where You dwell." Psalm 42:3 NIV

When would I feel like the old me again? Why had my joy disappeared?

The period of despair that had taken over my life sent me spiraling into a deep, dark hole and I couldn't seem to climb out.

I was living through a drought. To be honest, I didn't know when or if, I would regain my strength or get my joy back. I had lost my grip on my once-so-normal life.

Somewhere on my journey through life I got distracted and lost my way. I could never put my finger on why it happened but my spiral caused doom, gloom and discouragement to wash over me in relentless waves.

It was a combination of things. My workload was huge and honestly, some of that was my fault. I'm a perfectionist and that can consume a person. I wanted to be a good wife, mother, teacher, friend, and co-worker. I wanted to take care of everyone.

But I wasn't taking care of me.

I felt like I was walking around in a fog. I wanted to sleep all of the time, I didn't have any energy, and I didn't want to be responsible-- FOR ANYTHING.

That's pretty tough to do when you're a wife, a mom to a young teenage daughter, working a full-time job, and committed to a number of extra activities.

It may have been 18 years ago, but it only takes a moment to remember the sadness, the overwhelm, and the tired. I was in a dark place and I felt like I was there alone.

I did my best to hide what was going on in my own life from my family and my colleagues. I believed I could work my way through it. After all, this kind of thing doesn't happen to someone who is always in control, always in charge of a schedule, and always tending to others.

One memory stands out in my mind. I did NOT want to start school that fall. I kept toying with the idea of resigning my teaching position and being a stay-at-home mom. That was not what my husband wanted to hear, and truth be told, it sounded nothing like me. And he just kept asking why and wondering what I would do if I walked away from my mission field.

I didn't have an answer for him. I just kept trying to rationalize and justify my thought process.

I felt desolate and disconnected from God, and with that kind of twisted thinking Satan tried to convince me that I wasn't worthy of His love and forgiveness. It seemed as if I had a thirst I couldn't quench. As if my lips were dry and cracked.

God knew what I was battling. While I was doing everything I could to hold my ground and withstand Satan's attacks, my faulty thinking and shortcomings were sinking me further and further into depths of despair and poor decision making.

As I tried to look ahead, I couldn't imagine anything getting better. I didn't know what God had in store for me. I turned to reading secular articles and books, trying to find a solution to take me from the darkness I was struggling in. Nothing provided the permanent relief I so desperately sought.

But one September day God intervened and sent an angel to my classroom door. I believe beyond a shadow of doubt she was working on His behalf to draw me out of the dry, sun-scorched land and lead me to a place where I could dwell in His truth to restore my joy.

I'm not sure why, but I poured out everything I was experiencing to my friend. But instead of judging me, she lovingly offered me Scripture. Verse after verse and example after example of God's love for me. She shared what happens when we don't tend to our hearts and minds. And then she prayed for me, and over me. She didn't stop there.

The next morning she came by my classroom with two devotions from one of her favorite books, 'Streams in the Desert,' by Charles Cowman.

She selected those passages specifically for what I was going through. For the first time in a long time I felt there was hope and a future. I am comforted by how Scripture tells me in Psalm 43:3 to let the *'Light guide me to the place where my Heavenly Father dwells.'*

The Apostle Paul, tells us in Romans 15:13, NIV, *"May the God of hope fill you with all joy and peace in believing, so that by the power of the Holy Spirit you may abound in hope."*

After being immersed in a thick and desperate darkness, my Redeemer provided a glorious light and rescue. He supplied the nourishment I so needed and it was through His timing and control that I would stand tall again and lean on his continual guidance to grow through

Him and in Him. My time with Him is my dwelling place. The place that prepares me to face my earthly responsibilities.

I walked through the physical, emotional, and mental turmoil for nine, long months. But because of God's grace and mercy I am able to share my hope with you today.

The angel God sent that day was not an overnight miracle, but instead she was a support system to walk with me through this journey. My heart was dry and needed tending, replenishing, and restoring as only the Master can do. He lovingly provided exactly what I needed.

How blessed I was then, and now, to receive His redeeming drops of grace that make the difference in my life.

God sustains us despite our circumstances. Even in dry places and in drought. He satisfies me and makes me stronger in the physical, emotional, and spiritual realms. God is my daily bread. So when you feel discouraged follow God's light and truth. He will be your guide forever and ever.

> MY TIME WITH GOD IS MY DWELLING PLACE. THE PLACE THAT PREPARES ME TO FACE MY EARTHLY RESPONSIBILITIES.

PRAYER: Dear Lord, I draw closer to You in prayer as I feel discouraged. Help me to lift my spirit and depend on Your Word for strength and comfort. I praise you for bringing me out of the darkness and into the light. Just like King David, I long to dwell in Your presence all the days of my life. I'm thankful for Your faithful care and provision that continues to lead me home to Your holy mountain. Amen.

1. How might seeking God's truth on a daily basis keep you on the right path?

2. Describe a time when you called out to God and needed to dwell in the House of the Lord.

3. Is anyone you know struggling? How might traveling alongside them and sharing God's Word help them?

Dwell in the Psalm

4. Name three ways you can clothe yourself with the Armor of God to stave off the enemy's assault?

Prayer Journal

Psalm 132:14

THiS iS my

resting place

READ

REFLECT

Dwell in the Psalms

RELATE

REMEMBER

PRAY

READ

REFLECT

RELATE

REMEMBER

PRAY

READ

REFLECT

RELATE

REMEMBER

PRAY

I LONG
TO
Dwell

IN YOUR TENT
FOREVER AND

TAKE REFUGE

IN THE

shelter

OF YOUR WINGS.

PSALM 61:4 NIV

WEEK TWO
Scripture Reading

1   PSALM 27:4

2   PSALM 37:27

3   PSALM 37:29

4   PSALM 37:3

5   PSALM 39:12

6   PSALM 43:3

7   PSALM 61:4

How to Dwell in Peace
WHEN YOU'VE BEEN SUCKER-PUNCHED

"How good and pleasant it is when God's people live together in unity!" Psalm 133:1 NIV

From a young age my parents taught me the 'Golden Rule.' When I think about God's word in Matthew 7:12 NASB, *"In everything, there fore, treat people the same way you want them to treat you, for thi is the Law and the Prophets,"* I am reminded to show the kind of lov to others that God shows me every day. But sometimes it isn't easy.

I haven't always been the recipient of someone else's love. In fact, there was the time when an acquaintance put me through a grueling test of love, grace, and forgiveness.

I'll never know why she chose to unleash her personal unhappiness upon me while sitting in a graduate school class surrounded by other professionals, but it happened.

And I never even saw it coming.

Our class was enjoying a break when she unloaded on me. Terrible words that were both personal and hurtful. The kind of words that disprove the old adage, 'Sticks and stones may break your bones, but words will never hurt you." Believe me, her words hurt all the way to my core.

As quickly as possible I left class, found the nearest restroom and sobbed. I didn't know what I had done to deserve this kind of treatment, but I knew I had to clean my face, return to class, and ride home in the same vehicle with her. Needless to say, we exchanged no words during the 40 minute drive. While I was stunned beyond comprehension, I knew I had to be very thoughtful about my next steps.

After a few days of sadness and grieving over the hurt and betrayal, I turned to Scripture and a godly friend to help me navigate the situation. I spent some time in meditation, dwelling on the comfort of God's Word.

While the situation caught me off guard, it taught me a valuable lesson about living together in unity. I learned that as difficult as the experience had been, I would not get even. Instead I needed to forgive her and love her, no matter what.

No matter the heart breaking words or the actions she displayed. No matter the shock and numbness I felt in the aftermath. No matter.

When we follow God our thoughts and actions ought to demonstrate our love for Him and our others.

I allowed God's Word to calm my heart and set me on the path to truth that was both comforting and affirming. In the days that followed I gained freedom from the harsh words, the disappointing behavior, and the painful hurt the prince of darkness tried to shackle me with.

Living the way God wants us to live is a decision we make. One of the things I've gleaned through studying Scripture is that God's laws are not burdensome. They are for my good and the good of everyone in my community. His instructions teach us how to live in peace and unity, even when we get sucker-punched.

Jesus sums up the entire law in His response to the scribes.

"The most important one," answered Jesus, "is this: 'Hear, O Israel: The Lord our God, the Lord is one. Love the Lord your God with all your heart and with all your soul and with all your mind and with all

your strength.' The second is this: 'Love your neighbor as yourself.
'There is no commandment greater than these." (Mark 12:29-31, NIV)

There is the indisputable truth. We are to offer to others what God gives to us. To love others as Christ loves us proves that our heart, mind, soul and strength are transformed by His love.

This woman wasn't my sister or a trusted friend, or even my next door neighbor. But she was a colleague and despite the circumstances, God calls us to lavish undeserved favor on those who don't deserve it. Like He does for us. We all make mistakes that threaten how we love and care for others, but it's the lessons we learn that make the difference.

> THERE IS AN INDISPUTABLE TRUTH ... WE ARE TO OFFER TO OTHERS WHAT GOD GIVES TO US.

As I reflect back on this hurtful situation I am grateful for my reaction. Because I chose to love and forgive through Christ, this relationship has been restored. I have no doubt that when we fully love God with our whole being and care for others as we are supposed to, we fulfill the intent of the Ten Commandments and God's Laws in the Old Testament.

I have thanked God over and over again for the protection He provided that evening. My focus on Him kept me from lashing out and doing even more damage. Choosing to love others leads us to live together in unity and how much better and more pleasant that is than choosing retaliation.

Dwell in the Psalms

PRAYER: *Our dear Heavenly Father, I come to you today with love in my heart and hope for a better tomorrow. I pray for unity and restoration as I seek to forgive others who have hurt me. Father, I look to You to work in me and create a heart, mind, and soul that shows obedience and adoration. Thank you for commanding us to fully love others as You love us, because there is no commandment greater than these. In Your Precious Name I pray, Amen.*

1. What does Scripture say we should respond with when someone hurts us deeply?

2. Sometimes we believe we don't have much to offer for the cause of peace and unity, but God's Word tells us we do. How do you show the fullness of God's love to others, even in times of difficulty or distress?

3. What does it mean to you to live out God's love? How can you show others that God lives in us?

Dwell in the Psalms

Psalm 133:1

Prayer Journal

WHAT INSPIRED YOUR SOUL THIS WEEK?

READ

REFLECT

RELATE

REMEMBER

PRAY

READ

REFLECT

RELATE

REMEMBER

PRAY

READ

REFLECT

RELATE

REMEMBER

PRAY

Blessed

ARE THOSE WHO
DWELL IN
YOUR HOUSE
EVER SINGING
YOUR *Praise*

PSALM 84:4 ESV

WEEK THREE
Scripture Reading

15 PSALM 65:4

16 PSALM 68:6

17 PSALM 69:35-36

18 PSALM 84:10

19 PSALM 84:4

20 PSALM 85:9

21 PSALM 87:2

Dwelling in the Presence of God
WHEN YOU HAVE A BUSY LIFE

"The one thing I ask of the LORD--the thing I seek most--is to live in the house of the LORD all the days of my life, delighting in the LORD's perfections and meditating in his Temple." Psalm 27:4 NLT

I recently had lunch with a group of friends when I stopped to listen to the conversation buzz. Everyone at the table was sharing how busy they were.

One friend said, "I can't seem to get everything done. No matter how hard I try I can't get caught up and I'm running on fumes." Another added, "There's no time for my family, and my kids are constantly on the go. I don't have a minute to breathe, much less do anything for me."

For all I knew we should have been wearing our 'Super Girl' capes to that lunch. There we were trying to be all and do it all. But one thing seemed to be missing: any desire to bring these crazy schedules to a screeching halt and be still.

Many times our overload problems are self-induced. We believe everybody needs our help and if we want something done right, then we have to do it ourselves. Maybe it's our desire to be super woman that makes our hands shoot straight up in the air and scream, "I'll do it!"

While we may believe we're doing good works, the behavior is not what God wants. It's time to admit that we operate beyond our capacity and are simply trying to do too much. As Glynnis Whitwer shares in her book, Taming the TO-DO List, *"Our expectations about our time and energy are simply unrealistic. We're like Cinderella's stepsisters trying to squeeze our feet into that glass slipper."*

While most of us can identify with an overwhelmed schedule, I have seen first hand the potential harm a hectic lifestyle can bring without Christ as the center.

Many of us have found ourselves in similar situations, so why do we continue to sacrifice our quiet time with the Lord for unrest and upheaval? Wouldn't it make more sense to spend time in worship and equip ourselves with the Word of God so that we could bear the load and manage the unmanageable? Time spent well with the Lord seems to put everything else in perspective.

If my precious friends were grappling with major time constraints and busyness, I wondered if they were getting the spiritual nourishment they so needed? Did they have any idea the difference it would make?

Because even when I'm on overload (it happens more than I want), I have learned to relinquish the stress and the non-stop pace to God because I know I can trust Him to help me navigate the challenges.

> TIME SPENT WELL WITH THE LORD PUTS EVERYTHING ELSE INTO PERSPECTIVE.

In Psalm 27:4, David reminds us that his greatest pleasure was to live in God's presence each day of his life. Although David struggled with situations and made mistakes just like us, his priority remained the same: *to seek God continually and dwell in His house all the days of his life.*

If we find ourselves saying over and over that we are too busy, then something has to change. And change now. Ask yourself what commitments are necessary and what motivating factors cause you to keep adding to your already busy schedule.

We should pray continually about our priorities and seek God before we choose any extra stuff.

"If any of you lacks wisdom, you should ask God, Who gives generously to all without finding fault, and it will be given to you. But when you ask, you must believe and not doubt, because the one who doubts is like a wave of the sea, blown and tossed by the wind." (James 1:5-6, NIV)

These verses provide us with the instructions to ask God for wisdom to know what to do. Whatever we choose should always align with God's Word and His character.

If we truly long to get away from the bustling world, then we should seek opportunities to meet God in His dwelling place, His holy temple. It's there we can lay the chaos aside, turn to God to help us quietly meditate and pray, and receive His wisdom for our lives.

So figure out what you really need to be doing. Stop the crazy, overwhelmed life. Say NO and mean it. Prioritize and make your to-do list meaningful, manageable and heart felt. Moments with your children or family members can't be replaced by spending time on assignments meant for other people.

Remember, *we can meet God anywhere, at any time.*

1. Consider what contributed to your overwhelm. What motivated your decisions to say yes to too much? What could you have done differently?

2. God wants you to rest in Him. Repeating and personalizing these words from Psalm 4:8 NIV may bring comfort: "In peace I will lie down and sleep, for you alone, Lord, make me dwell in safety."

3. What changes can you make to slow your hectic lifestyle?

Prayer: Lord, I come to You seeking Your presence in my life and wanting to dwell in Your house all the days of my life. I want to rest in Your assurances that I can create a schedule that is pleasing to You and my family. I pray for wisdom as I make decisions and I ask for Your mercy and grace as I choose what is best for me and my family in the long run, and not what will make me look good in the present. Thank You for Your redeeming grace. In Your Name I pray. Amen.

Prayer Journal

READ

REFLECT

RELATE

REMEMBER

PRAY

READ

REFLECT

RELATE

REMEMBER

PRAY

READ

REFLECT

RELATE

REMEMBER

PRAY

whoever
DWELLS IN THE
Shelter OF
THE MOST HIGH
WILL *Rest*
IN THE SHADOW OF
THE ALMIGHTY

PSALM 91:1 NIV

WEEK FOUR
Scripture Reading

22 PSALM 91:1

23 PSALM 98:7

24 PSALM 101:6

25 PSALM 101:7

26 PSALM 107:35-37

27 PSALM 125:1

28 PSALM 132:14

How to Dwell in the Spirit
WHEN DISAPPOINTMENT STRIKES

"Hear my prayer, Lord; let my cry for help come to you. Do not hide your face from me when I am in distress. Turn your ear to me; when I call, answer me quickly. " Psalm 42:3 NIV

It seems like a lifetime ago when I felt God calling me to step out of the classroom and make the move to school administration.

I completed all the coursework and developed a focused plan of action to ensure I would be ready. I got the first job quickly and promoted from one position to the next, believing along the way that God had placed me right where I needed to be to one day lead a school district.

I laid out every painstaking detail it would take to compete for a top school district position. I even went so far as to tell God that I had a 10 year time frame to achieve this promotion destination or time would run out.

God laughed. I didn't hear Him at first because I was busy making my plans and asking Him to bless them.

As I garnered the necessary experiences to be qualified for a top spot I paid close attention to nearby districts with openings, where I would potentially be a good fit. While I was searching for just the place God needed me, I was also fervently praying to not have to move away from my family, my home city, my aging mother, my friends, or my church. I really did believe God would provide an opportunity close to home, as I was not willing to sacrifice what I had for what I wanted.

So when an opportunity presented itself nearby I took a chance.

I strongly considered my favorable relationship with the district, but I also knew there were extraneous things going on behind the scenes that I had little knowledge of, nor any control over.

I pressed on, weighing the pro's and con's of the position. I continued to pray about it and made the decision to go through the paperwork process, submit the application packet and wait.

"For I know the plans I have for you," says the Lord. "They are plans for good and not for disaster, to give you a future and a hope." Jeremiah 29:11 NIV

I received a phone call for a first round interview. It came and went; all pretty general stuff, but there were a few pointed questions I knew had underlying meanings.

The next week I received a second call saying I was one of the three finalists for the position. Even with my 'not so good feeling,' I remained optimistic. The door was open and I would be obedient and walk through it.

From the moment the first question was asked that evening, nothing was as it should have been. I left the interview knowing I would not be the candidate of choice. Confirmation came a few days later. I was disappointed of course, as this position was something I had worked for and wanted, but one of the lessons we learn early on in life is that we don't get everything we want.

I still cried out to the Lord asking, *"Why did You let me walk through every single door and not give it to me?"*

After a few days of replaying the sequence of events and wondering why I hadn't gotten the job, I began to realize what God wanted me to learn through all of this. It was as if He said, "Mitzi, what were you thinking?"

God knew I would be disappointed, but ultimately He had a different plan. It was through my season of setback that He revealed what He wanted me to uncover through this process. He wanted me to experience first hand the situation I would be in and recognize it was not what I needed. He wanted me to see it was not the place for me. Even these revelations didn't keep me from being sad and feeling frustrated.

When disappointment strikes we have decisions to make. I could have become discouraged and lost my way. I could have turned my back on God believing He failed me. I could have made the decision not to continue pursuing future opportunities for advancement. But what would I have gained from believing these mistruths?

> IT'S ALL ABOUT CHOOSING TO DWELL IN THE PRESENCE OF GOD DESPITE OUR DISAPPOINTMENTS.

That's how the enemy misleads us to believe his lies. He plants seeds of doubt. He wants us to believe that circumstances, failures, and successes define us. He wants us to believe that we have been ripped off, short changed, and wronged.

None of that is truth.

Disappointments happen to all of us and they are a part of life. Just look at David, Moses, Hannah, Job, Sarah, and others, who experienced setback after setback, and yet continued to be faithful and trust God.

There is no sin in feeling let down. It's how we handle disappointment that makes the difference. It's about holding up in the midst of adversity. It's about dealing with disappointments, big and small, and rebounding to see God's hand of protection in all we do. It's about choosing to dwell in the presence of God despite our disappointments.

"May the beloved of the Lord dwell in security by Him, "Who shields him all the day, And he dwells between His shoulders."
Deuteronomy 33:12 NASB

God used this situation to breathe new life into me and point me in the direction of His plan for me to pursue.

In the midst of the disappointment I realized interacting with students and teachers in the classroom was exactly what I needed to continue doing, and surprisingly, what I wanted to do. I also needed to remember that *while things did not go the way I had planned, they did go the way I had prayed.* God's wild pursuit down this path had a completely different destination than I expected and I have so much to be grateful for.

PRAYER: Heavenly Father, I come to you asking You to hold me close as I weather the storms. Sometimes when disappointment gets in the way of my hopes and dreams I suffer an emotional setback and tears. I know Your plans for my life are far beyond what I could ever imagine. I want to draw closer to you, seeking Your strength and comfort along the way. Like so many other times I long to dwell in Your presence all the days of my life. I'm thankful for Your faithfulness. Amen.

1. Consider a time when you faced disappointment. How did you handle it?

2. Looking back can you see what God might have been trying to teach you?

3. Is there something you are hoping for or working toward today? What steps can you take to protect your heart from disappointment?

Dwell in the Psalms

4. How will you plan to dwell with God instead of disengaging from Him if things don't work out like you planned?

5. How will you put into practice what you've learned?

Prayer Journal

Psalm 84:4

READ

REFLECT

RELATE

REMEMBER

PRAY

READ

REFLECT

RELATE

REMEMBER

PRAY

READ

REFLECT

RELATE

REMEMBER

PRAY

Bible Art Journaling

SCRIPTURE MEMORY CARDS — copy, cut out, display or keep with you to help memorize God's Word.

I LOVE YOUR *sanctuary* LORD THE PLACE WHERE *Your* GLORIOUS PRESENCE *dwells.*

PSALM 26:8 NLT

I LONG TO *Dwell* IN YOUR TENT FOREVER AND TAKE REFUGE IN THE *shelter* OF YOUR WINGS.

PSALM 61:4 NIV

whoever DWELLS IN THE *Shelter* OF THE MOST HIGH WILL *Rest* IN THE SHADOW OF THE ALMIGHTY

PSALM 91:1 NIV

Blessed ARE THOSE WHO DWELL IN YOUR HOUSE EVER SINGING YOUR *Praise*

PSALM 84:4 ESV

Dwell in the Psalms

BIBLE MARGIN TEMPLATE / BOOKMARK — color, copy or cut out and add to your journaling page as a tip-in or trace / draw design directly into your Journaling Bible's margin.

One thing I have DESIRED from the LORD THAT I may Dwell IN THE HOUSE OF the LORD all the days of my life

Psalm 27:4

TRACEABLE WORDS / PHRASES — trace these words / phrases directly into your Bible or journal or use as a visual guide to practice your creative lettering.

JOURNALING CARDS — color, copy or cut out and add to your journaling page as a tip-in or add to a blank card and send someone a note of encouragement.

THAT'S A WRAP

Soul Friends, thank you for joining us to spend time in God's Word to grow in our understanding of how important is it to make it a priority to dwell with God. Oh He longs to spend time with us! And in this precious personal one-on-one time is when our soul deep relationship with our Heavenly Father is grown.

> ## PSALM 119:147-148
> ## I RISE BEFORE DAWN & CRY FOR HELP;
> ## I HOPE IN YOUR WORDS.
> ## MY EYES ARE AWAKE
> ## BEFORE THE WATCHES OF THE NIGHT,
> ## THAT I MAY MEDITATE ON YOUR PROMISE.

Friends, let's make spending time with God a daily priority and set our hearts and minds on the beautiful heavenly things above.

As we go forward ...

Let's hold on to the truths from God's Word about His faithfulness and continue to pray with the expectation of God delivering an answer to our prayers.

Blessings Soul Friends

Meet the Authors

Mitzi Neely encourages and inspires women of all ages through her teachings on grace, love, joy and peace, while thriving in the world we live in. Her heart is to lighten your load, while conveying her message that nobody's perfect. Her desire when she speaks, sings, creates or instructs is honesty and transparency, such that God receives glory and honor.

To connect with Mitzi, visit www.PeacefullyImperfect.net or email her directly at peacefullyimperfect@gmail.com. You can find her on Twitter @a_joyfulpeace and on her Facebook page, Peacefully Imperfect.

Additional Resources from *Peacefully Imperfect Ministries*

Devotional Book
A Thankful Heart: 30 Days to the Grateful Life

A Thankful Heart: 30 Days to the Grateful Life Bonus Kit
Scripture Reading Plan ~ Scripture Cards
Illustration Printables
30 Day Thankful Heart Challenge Journal

Nourish the Soul
30 Day Scripture Reading Plans and
Encouragement / Prayer calendars
Unshakeable Love ~ Spiritual Growth
Declutter the Soul ~ Hope for the Soul
Criticism and Challenges ~ Joy-Filled Life
Relax, Refresh, Replenish ~ Anxiety and Fear

Eight Truths About Happiness Mini-Bible Study

20 Ways to Beat the Blues Study Packet
Scripture Reading Plan ~ 20 Ways to Beat the Blues
Scripture Cards

For more information visit:
PeacefullyImperfect.net

Jana Kennedy-Spicer is a wife, mom and Nana who is passionate about inspiring and encouraging women on their daily walk with Christ. A woman rescued and repaired by the grace of God, she loves to share about the realness of God's love, redemption and faithfulness. Embarking on a new life journey, she is dedicated to using her blogging, Bible teaching, writing, drawing, painting and graphic designs to bring glory to the Lord.

Jana teaches Bible Study and Bible Journaling in the Dallas, Texas area. To connect with Jana, visit www.SweetToTheSoul.com or email her directly at jana@sweettothesoul.com.

FB: Sweet To The Soul   and   Sweet To The Soul Shoppe
IG: jana_sweettothesoul and sweettothesoulshoppe
PIN: SweetToTheSoul

Additional Resources from *Sweet To The Soul Ministries*

31-Day Devotionals
Let Your Light Shine : Being a Light in a Dark World

31-Day Scripture Journals
New Life ~ Love Is ~ Grace ~ I Believe
God's Masterpiece ~ Let Your Light Shine ~ Anchored Hope
Everyday Thanksgiving

Coloring Books
Garden of Life ~ Love One Another
Bearing Fruit ~ Coloring the Scriptures

Bible Study Journals
Bearing Fruit ~ Inspiring Women
I Am Not Alone ~ Gracious Words
Everyday Thanksgiving ~ You Are So Loved

Bible Journaling Templates /
Color Your Own Bookmarks

Color Pages & Prints

Bible Journaling / Crafting Digital Kits
Gods' Masterpiece ~ Bearing Fruit ~ Gifts of the Heart
You Are So Loved ~ New Life ~ Freedom in Christ

For more information visit: SweetToTheSoul.com/Soul-Inspired

Visit our Etsy shop at www.SweetToTheSoulShoppe.com

Devotionals and Journals also available at www.Amazon.com

Made in the USA
Las Vegas, NV
07 March 2021